Bloom Forever

~Poetry Journal~

Cynthia M. Lamb

Amani Publishing, LLC

Barbara Joe Williams

Tallahassee, FL

Copyright © 2013 by Cynthia M. Lamb
Bloom Forever

Amani Publishing, LLC
P. O. Box 12045
Tallahassee, FL 32317
(850) 264-3341

A company based on faith, hope, and love

Visit our website at: **www.barbarajoe.webs.com**

Email us at: **amanipublishing@aol.com**

ISBN: 978098336638

LCCN: 2012955598

Cover photo courtesy of: Bigstockphoto.com

Cover creation by: Diane Bass

Dedicated to my daughter, *Dahlia*.

Your birth taught me my greatest earthly love:
Motherhood.

Thank you for inspiring me to live my best life with your presence,
your inquisitiveness, and your love.

May your quest for Love be Beautiful and thorn-free.
May God Bless your Journey and your Life.

Love and Blessings Always,

Mami

FORWARD
By L. B. Lamb

Love is reflected in love. And life is the mirror where love is reflected. The poetic reflections of Ms. Portalatín's* life are blinding in their brilliance.

Her life's journey has been blessed with a richness of relationships, loves experienced, and loves lost.

I invite you to share... to enjoy... to feel the magical ways love has led this gifted poet to reach inside of herself and find the spirit to grow in love in a sometimes frightening world. To find the confidence to love herself. To be the person she truly is... a magnificent reflection of God's Love.

Her poetry is an abundant reflection of a lifelong journey which has led her to find true love of life, and in life, as a result of the pursuit of God in her life. The rich diversity in style and substance of her writings captures her deep emotional journey to happiness and spiritual light.

It has been one of my life's greatest blessings that Cynthia has chosen to share her life's journey as expressed through her poetry.

I am sure that the verses offered in this publication will help you to trust your emotions, will lift your spirit, and give you pause for faith, as it has for me.

Thank you, Cynthia!

(*Portalatín is the author's maiden name, under which she wrote most of her poetry until she and Lonnie married in 2012.)

###

If I were the wind
You and I would fly across the oceans
We would understand the Seas
And every moment

If life were the wind
We'd fly always
Life would go by without us knowing
Where would time go?
Would there be such a thing?

We would enjoy every moment
From such a heavenly view

L. L.

###

- Poem by: Lonnie B. Lamb -

A few kind words...

"I've known Cynthia for a few years, and there was a connection upon meeting her. We both have a love for writing, and she would contribute to a few of my projects as well as serve as my copy-editor. Having said that, what you're about to read is the heart of Cynthia. *Bloom Forever's* poetry will cause you to laugh, cry, and reflect the pages of your life. May the words you read touch your life in a special way."

Tremayne Moore, Maynetre Manuscripts, LLC.
Author and publisher of the three-part, *Take It From*, poetic verse series and the novel, *Deaf Dumb Blind & Stupid – Michael Anderson's Fight for Life.*

Looking for me?

This is a place I'd been for a long time... "Looking for me." Finding, accepting and loving "me" has been a life-long process, and at forty-four, I am still evolving. In my experiences with romantic love, and in life, I have found writing to be therapeutic. It has also helped me find "me." Throughout life's struggles, love conquers fear, even in my darkest hours. When I feel like giving up, love and faith keep me hopeful... and I live to love another day, thanks to God's amazing grace.

At times, my search for love led me to unhappy and difficult places. God, in His infinite mercy, held me through it all, despite my awkward steps, and I am thankful for the love He gives me unconditionally.

If you've ever felt rejected, you might not say "loving is easy." Yet, I encourage you to **Give Love**, no matter the circumstance. As a good friend once told me, **love is a verb**. And from my experience, I know it will always return... it will always bloom.

This book is a compilation of twenty-plus years of my "love journey" with all its painful and glorious experiences. Some poems are in "raw" form, scribbles and all – wonderfully imperfect, like me. The book's title symbolizes what I believe love does in each of us when nurtured.

A few THANK YOU's to those who inspired and helped me in finally compiling my poems:

- **Jesus –** my Lord & Savior... **He loved me first.**

- **Lonnie B. Lamb –** my wonderful husband, for believing in me and my dreams. Thank you for loving and growing with me.

- **Tremayne Moore** – for encouraging my writing efforts and including me in your works... thanks for the extra push.

- **Thomas J. Scurlock** – for lending your ear and helping me laugh through my foibles. Thanks for your forever friendship and thanks for the toaster, Ha Ha!

- **Barbara Joe Williams** – for your enthusiasm, kind advice, and for publishing my first book. Thanks for creating the Tallahassee Authors Network to help writers connect.

- **Family and Friends** – too many to list... I love you mucho. **<3**

As you read this book, I thank **You** for taking time to walk with me in my poetic journey. May God bless and keep you always, and may you "Bloom Forever" in Love.

-Cynthia M. Lamb

Poems:

1. Love in the Wind (1985)
2. I Can't Recall (1985)
3. Eyes Clear Blue (1985)
4. Daydreamer (1986)
5. Knight Love (July 1986)
6. Questions (July 1986)
7. An answer (August 1986)
8. Poems of the Mind (August 1986)
9. Fair (Fall 1986)
10. Goodbye (Fall 1986)
11. Walking (Fall 1986)
12. Control or Submission (Winter 1986)
13. In Comes the Tide (1986)
14. Heartache (Fall 1987)
15. Put Up or Give Up (1987)
16. What's Done Is Done (September 1987)
17. New Love (October 1987)
18. Echo (December 1987)
19. Foolish tears (December 1987)
20. Guilt in Love (December 1987)
21. Incompatible (December 1987)
22. In Love Twice (December 1987)
23. The Joker and the Princess (December 1987)
24. Dreaming (January 1988)
25. Saddest Thing (January 1988)
26. A Special Prayer (1988)
27. Jehová Reina (February 3, 1998)
28. Con Cristo Viviré (March 19, 1988)
29. Te Seguiré, Te Serviré (April 16, 1988)
30. Baby Love (Spring 1988)
31. I Could (June 1988)
32. Runaway (Summer 1988)

33. *Yea Yea (July 1988)*
34. *Time to Grow (July 1988)*
35. *Whispering Wind (August 1988)*
36. *Thoughts of a Learned Novice (September 27, 1988)*
37. *¿Que Quiere La Bella? (December 3, 1989)*
38. *Card Game (December 1989)*
39. *Pearl (Circa 1990)*
40. *Sin Reproches (February 24, 1990)*
41. *Finding Gold (July 24, 1990)*
42. *Haunting Memories (July 25, 1990)*
43. *Silent Treatment (November 10, 1990)*
44. *Tears for a Lullaby (January 5, 1991)*
45. *Love (July 2, 1991)*
46. *Bathroom (July 4, 1991)*
47. *Living or Dreaming (July 6, 1991)*
48. *Excuse Me (March 19, 1992)*
49. *Yugoslavia (July 21, 1992)*
50. *Soul, Sista (November 7, 1992)*
51. *And we talked (December 8, 1992)*
52. *Seashells by the Sea (December 8, 1992)*
53. *Coco Loco (Winter 1992)*
54. *I in Me (February 25, 1993)*
55. *Woman (March 6, 1993)*
56. *I Love You, Still (March 1993)*
57. *Phobias (April 23, 1993)*
58. *Was There Love (June 13, 1993)*
59. *Sit Still Says the Lord (August 29, 1993)*
60. *Let Me Know (November 8, 1993)*
61. *Olas de Amor (November 17, 1993)*
62. *A Mother's Dreams (February 6, 1994)*
63. *Looking for me? (March 2, 1994)*
64. *Richmond (June 25, 1994)*
65. *It's a Shame (July 19, 1994)*
66. *Wrong Timing (August 9, 1994)*
67. *This Moment (August 12, 1994)*
68. *Say I Do (August 12, 1994)*

69. One Day (August 12, 1994)

70. Burned (August 18, 1994)

71. The Dream (August 24, 1994)

72. AJP (August 31, 1994)

73. Fabrizzio (September 26, 1994)

74. Paper Dreams (October 1, 1994)

75. Ticho (October 1994)

76. Hardened (October 22, 1994)

77. Waffle House Friend (November 6, 1994)

78. Hawk (November 9, 1994)

79. Angel (November 14, 1994)

80. Car of My Dreams (November 14, 1994)

81. Morning (March 19, 1995)

82. The War Within (April 19, 1995)

83. Bus Depot Dream (April 1995)

84. Fear (April 23, 1995)

85. Living (April 25, 1995)

86. Queasy Feeling (June 9, 1995)

87. In Love (February 14, 1996)

88. Enamorada (February 1996)

89. Viento de Amor (November 14, 1996)

90. Poema Para Vivir (August 12, 2000)

91. Worn and Loved (July 9, 2001)

92. Early morning ramblings (January 14, 2006)

93. The Flame (August 26, 2006)

94. Waiting (March 3, 2007)

95. A Prayer for Strength (April 16, 2007)

96. The Kiln (April 19, 2007)

97. High Tide, New Horizon (September 21, 2007)

98. Lies (December 1, 2007)

99. I Paint (March 9, 2008)

100. On the Eve of Dawn (August 5, 2008)

101. Still (December 12, 2008)

102. Caught (February 5, 2009)

103. Clarity (December 3, 2009)

Love in the Wind

It's summer again,
I'm with my friends.
Thinking of the sun,
wanta have some fun.
If you were here, we'd be feeling free;
running with the wind, you and me.

Life is short, life is sweet.
The thrill of life, we cannot beat.
Solving mysteries in our mind,
our life begins to unwind.

If you were here,
I'd hold you near;
I'd let you know that you were dear.
But now you've gone
far past my way;
I wish I'd had the guts to say
That you were dear
when you were here,
so I could now hold you near.

True love lasts.
Lust goes fast.
Love endures,
and it cures,
all our ails;
it never fails.

1985

I Can't Recall

Hello, it's good to see you again,
you haven't changed a lot.
I remember all the love and joy,
the happiness you brought.

But I can't recall anything at all
that'd lead me to believe
someday you would leave.

I see you now before my eyes,
Oh how could I have known
you'd fool me with your grand disguise,
you'd leave me on my own.

I can't recall
anything at all
that'd lead me to believe
someday you would leave.

I tried for sometime to find a reason,
but you never gave a clue.
I guess our love was out of season,
but I never, never knew.

And I can't recall
anything at all
that'd lead me to believe
somday you would leave.

Now it took a while to feel again,
but honey, I survived.
I'd gone too long without a friend,
but I still had my pride.

As you leave for the second time,
my mind and heart close a door.
I recognize one final sign:
I don't love you anymore.

1985

Eyes Clear Blue

It's been so long since I've thought of you
Since I've heard this song
But now I see your eyes clear blue
It was so wrong

Happiness knows no tears,
I never thought I'd fear
the day you went and left he here alone.

It took a while to live again
I never thought the pain would end
But now I'm free, can't you see
I'm not alone.

I've learned to find myself again
The sadness finally came to end
I'm free from you
Eyes clear blue

It's been so long sice I've thought of you
Since I've heard this song

I'm free from you. . . eyes clear blue.

1985

"DAYDREAMER"

I knew it from the start.
Your smile went to my heart.
Sweet dreams would soon appear.
Kept thinking you were near.
One look and I was "caught".
But fall in love I aught not,
For strangers never meet;
Crowds fade into the street.
But your face still remains,
And now it never rains.
Could it be true
I've fallen in love with you?
Some fate from the skies
Has binded us with ties
That will not be broken
Bye mere words spoken.
Sweet dreams reappear
Are you really near?
My heart begins to ache,
As suddenly I awake
To find that you are far
I wonder where you are.
Into your world you've gone
And my life must go on.
We're strangers who won't meet,
As you fade into the street.
And my dreams reappear,
For another prince is here.
Daydreamer,
Nightdreamer,
I'm a dreamer just like you.
Daydreamer,
Nightdreamer,
nothing I can do.
I'm a dreamer, just like you.

1986

Knight Love

Castles in the sky
Angels flying high
A knight in shinning armour
From darkness comes a murmur
Through the clouds appear
A lover with a spear.
Through my heart it goes
Taking with my life my woes
In the midst a soul
An angel becoming whole
The shine of a white dove
Is the magical light of love
Hear the beautiful music from afar
Becoming one with the brightest star
Lost are we forever
Who cannot be together

July 1986 – Florida

Questions

WHAT AM I TO DO;
WHAT AM I TO BE?
WHAT DREAMS OF MINE'LL COME TRUE;
WHAT IS THERE LEFT FOR ME TO SEE?

ONE PART OF ME SAYS, "GET OUT ON YOUR OWN".
ONE PART OF ME ASKS, "HOW?"
ONE PART OF ME IS AFRAID TO BE ALONE;
THE OTHER SAYS, "JUST GO, NOW!"

July 1986

"AN AMSWER"

Answers are there for the givers.
The questions remain for the takers.
You are free when your heart can see
that answers aren't hard to find.
Hearts are never blind.

****

August 1986

Poems of the Mind

Poems of the mind,
Sometimes unkind.
A story to be told.
Thoughts unfold.
Wanting to know,
Where to go.
Wanting to be.
Wanting to flee. . .
Wanting to stay,
Finding a way.

Poems of the mind,
Sometimes kind.
Wanting to be pure.
Finding a cure.
Living a lie. . .
watching the days go by.
Living a lie. . .
watch as time goes by.
Time passes by.
Love is life. . .
Is life love?

August 1986

Fair

Fall 86

"life is unfair
        to the kind.
life is fair
        to the blind."

Fall 1986

Goodbye

I can't read your eyes
all I hear are goodbyes
Hiding behind a mask of pride
The words sail with the sea's tide
But, the water is clear
They are pools of fear
The words you say,
the stories you tell. . .
They make me pray
for that water's well.
My words are dear,
but you can't hear. . .

Fall 1986

Walking

```
        . . . And  I  walk  alone.

Time  passes  so  slowly. . .

              but  I  walk  on. . .
```

Fall 1986 – Tallahassee, FL

Control or Submission

She's dressed all in black,
the color of control.
She's set out to find
one to make her whole.

That someone she seeks
lives deep in the night,
And when the two meet,
everything feels right.

By day she wears white
and a smile of submission.
By night she's another,
her face mirroring passion.

This woman who seemingly has it all,
drops everything for the night's call.
She cannot change, for her ways are set...
He dries the tears of a face that's not wet.

Winter 1986

In Comes the Tide

```
A SOLEMN FACE
A TRACE OF HUMAN KINDNESS
A SMILE
IS IT FOR THE MINDLESS
COLORS COLLIDE
IN COMES THE TIDE
TO WASH AWAY THE SHAME
AND THE PRIDE
SO THE SANDS CAN COMBINE
TO MAKE THIS WORLD DIVINE
```

1986

Heartache

?????????????????????????????????????
    What do you do when there's
Nothing left in your heart
    When you've given all the
Löve you can give
    How can you regain what you
Felt at the start
    When love gave you the
Only reason to live. . .
???

Fall 1987

Put Up or Give Up

Don't tell me lies over the phone.
Don't tell me that you're all alone.
You sounded so different tonight.
But, I'm not gonna put up a fight.

You'd been asleep, but sounded so awake.
My voice starts to tremble, inside I shake.
An old friend came to see you;
I wanted to believe you.
Or is she now in your bed,
hearing all that you've said?

It's alright to feel lonely, 'cause so have I;
so why do I feel like I just want to cry?
Because I can't stand to think she might've won,
that you'd given in or could've succumbed
to that lonely feeling that's so hard to fight
and forgotten your promises to me for a night.

I'm hurting so bad inside; I'm so full of doubt.
I want to believe that you'd never turn me out.
But you're so far away and I'm so alone
I can't feel your love on a long-distance phone.
I don't want to hear that you love me over the wire,
I want to rejoin you in an embrace of our fire.

If it's true that you're not all alone
Don't worry babe, I should've known.
All the hurt and pain I feel now
Will dissipate someway, somehow.
My eyes are closed, their shut so tight
'cause babe, I'm trying oh so hard to fight
This feeling twisting up my heart.
It's tearing my insides all apart.

Your voice sounded so strange and far tonight.
I wonder if I should just give up the fight?

1987

"WHAT'S DONE IS DONE"

What's done is done;
look on to what's to come.
Don't worry about the past
or what you did last.
Let the leaves fall where they may,
so that you can go on to another day.
Dream of the beautiful joys of tomorrow,
and do not dwell on yesterday's sorrow;
for what's done is done,
and can be changed by none.

Happiness felt now is as real as forever.
Sadness felt then can return never,
if let to remain where it belongs:
in the chorus of life's sad songs.
So always remember, if you fear
that something past has brought a tear. . .
forget thy sorrow, little one,
for what's done is done.

September 1987

"NEW LOVE"

Lying beside you, I feel so secure.
This love that I feel is real; I'm sure.
Never before has it felt so right
as it does here with you tonight.
Your heart beats so fast, and I'm almost afraid;
does it hold a place for me in the plans you've made?
Just before twelve you hurry me home,
and I'm left to spend the night alone.

It's two A M as I lie in bed;
I smile in remembrance of what you said. . .
Morning finds it still on my face,
where your kisses left their loving trace.
Joy fills my heart, and I shine with glee,
as I open the door and it's you that I see.
No doubt in my mind that you shall be
the one true love to set my heart free.

What started in a rush
has left me in a flush.
Emotions overriding;
got me out of hiding.

Should we take it slow,
or just go with the flow?
It's obvious where the answer lies;
just look into the glow of our eyes.

This love that started with such a spark
shall keep us warm throughout the dark.
And I'm so glad, for what we feel
is altogether, so forever real.

October 1987

Echo

Hello love, how have you been?
I guess you could say we didn't win.
The love we had was something new;
I'd never felt what I felt for you.
They say young love never dies,
but we know that's just lies.
If let, it fades away so fast!
All that's left are memories passed.

I've been alright living on my own,
but the nights find me cold and alone.
You say your days are full of new joys,
and your nights with laughter and noise,
that you've grown and no longer are the boy
who used to treat me like a toy.
Well, I'm no longer so young and naive;
I find your words a little hard to believe.

Were the pastures we both sought
as green as we would've thought?
Or has disallusion laced
the journeys we've traced?
Is it too late to make a start
after being so long apart?
I ask you again how you've been;
you echo my thoughts with a grin. . .

December 1987

FOOLISH TEARS

FOOLISH TEARS
I'VE CRIED IN VAIN
TEARS OF FEAR
ALL IN YOUR NAME

NO MORE TEARS FOR YOU I'LL CRY
NO MORE WILL I WONDER WHY
NO MORE NIGHTS LYING AWAKE
NO MORE FOOLISH HEART ACHE

TEARS I'VE SHED
ALONE IN BED
TEARS I'LL DISMISS
WITH ANOTHER'S KISS

THE DOOR TO TEARS I'VE LOCKED
NO MORE SHELTERED, DESPERATE THOUGHT
LET QUESTIONS UNANSWERED BE
DON'T WANNA KNOW, DON'T WANNA SEE

December 1987

Guilt in Love

Me and you--it feels like it's new,
but it's not the first time for me.

You think it'll last--you don't know my past,
and now I've just got to be free.

You'd never understand, that the touch of my hand
has been felt by another before.

It's best you don't know, so I think I'll just go.
I'm walking right on out the door.

We thought it was love, something sent from above,
but it didn't turn out that way.

You felt so secure, but I wasn't sure.
I'm telling you, I just can't stay.

The love that we had was made up of lies;
it's no wonder I couldn't look in your eyes.

It's so easy to deceive,
you never would believe.

You thought you were the only one to ever love me so,
but my heart had been claimed once some time ago.

And I just can't stand to see
that you've placed your faith in me,

when I couldn't trust you enough to say

that even though I loved you more,
I'd loved someone else before.

I was so glad that I'd found you.
I wanted to begin anew.

But baby, I can't take it anymore,
so move away from that door.

Baby, please just don't ask me why;
all I know is I've got to say goodbye.

December 1987

Incompatible

Physically speaking, we're compatible
Chemically speaking, it's undeniable
But listening to our conversation
brings about a revelation:
We're too set in our ways
We could change, but who says?
I'd love to spend my time with you
But that depends on what we'd do.
It's nice to stay at home at night
reading poems by candlelight
But after a while it starts to tire;
I need a night that's full of fire!
I like the feel of a crowd
with the music playing loud.
I like the feel of a beat
dancing underneath my feet!
You like the sound of a cello
playing tunes all too mellow.
You always fall asleep by eight
and think that I stay up too late.
After the moment's done you're tired.
You say I'm too lively, when I feel inspired.
I guess I'm too young; you don't understand,
I don't always want to be held by the hand.
I need to feel free, can't you see?
I'm my own person and want to be "me".
That doesn't mean that I don't care,
none like you could I find anywhere.
But don't try to hold me down to your side,
'cause it wouldn't be the first time I've defied
The love of a man who's tried to control
the reigns of this free-spirited soul.

December 1997

In Love Twice

How can you be in love twice?
You're breaking hearts, and
         that ain't nice.
Why couldn't one only suffice?
You're playing tricks with
         your own dice.
You're bound to lose and it's
         gonna hurt.
You're gonna wind up in the dirt.
You're gonna have to make up
         your mind,
Figure out which one's your kind.
If you play them on and on,
You'll wake up one day and
         they'll both be gone.
Now I know you love them
         both the same,
But girl, you better stop this
         game.
If you can't decide which one's
         for you,
Then find yourself another who'll do;
One who has what the other lacks.
Girl, you have to face up to
         the facts.

December 1987

"THE JOKER AND THE PRINCESS"

The joker doesn't know; the joker, he won't go.
The joker will cry, at every goodbye.
My little joker jokes; my little joker pokes.
My little joker kisses; my little joker misses.
My little joker wishes. . .

She will ellude; she'll sometimes act rude.
She may smile, but only for a while.
She knows just what to say, when he comes her way,
but doesn't know what to feel, for fear it'll become real.
He'll wonder, but won't ask,
for she hides behind a mask.
So he'll pretend to understand
with a touch of his hand.
But just a touch is all he'll get;
not more than that, you can bet.
And a touch doesn't last that long,
before he knows it, the princess is gone.

The joker will grieve, but he'll never leave.
He waits for a chance to renew the dance.
He'll smile and then cry, but won't say goodbye.
The joker, he'll live. . . and continue to give
his heart and soul away, to that princess every day.

She smiles with a tear, whispers words that are dear.
She's been crying ever since, she lost her only prince.
And now she can't go on, the days all seem so long.
Her heart aches in pain, as she calls out his name.
She dreams of a face, that none could replace.

The joker returns, but he never learns.
The joker, he just won't go; it's a shame he doesn't know.
The joker he kisses; the joker, he wishes. . .
the joker he misses.

December 1987

35   *Bloom Forever ~ by Cynthia M. Lamb*

Dreaming

If you could read my mind
you would think that I'm blind.

If you could hear what I think
you might think I'm on the brink.

But it's no secret, you see,
that I'm thinking of you and me.

Save all of your words of heed,
I won't listen, you're all I need.

Bubbles of song burst in my soul;
you're all I need to make me whole.

Can't you see what I mean?
Being with you is like a dream!

And I do believe that dreams come true
because I have someone like you.

Let me sleep forever in your eyes.
Keep me in this heavenly paradise.

This is where we both belong
and I want to dream on and on.

So when you see my eyes aglow,
all you really need to know

Is I won't ever leave you waiting,
doubting in me, or contemplating.

Know that what I feel is true
and that I'll never cease loving you.

January 1988

Saddest Thing

The saddest thing I ever heard
    was when you said
        goodbye.

The saddest thing I ever found
    was that it was
        a lie.

The bluest days I ever knew
    were those spent
        without you,

But what surprises me to hear
    is yours are gloomy,
        too!

I miss you more and more each day,
    but you could never
        know,

Because I'm too tied up in knots
    to ever let it
        show.

Let's give our love another chance,
    let's make a start
        again,

Go back in time to what we had
    and never let it
        end. . .

January 1988

"A Special Prayer"

A special prayer is in my heart.
It's singing thanks for this brand new
    start.
Without you, Lord, there'd be no way
that I'd be where I'm at today.
I still have long to reach my goal,
but with your love, my faith is
    whole.
I'm thankful for this chance to begin
on a new journey where I'm sure to
    win.
Where doubt once kept me from moving
along,
there now is a strength that carries
    me on.
No fears of what tomorrow will bring;
there's hope in my soul as I sing
this special prayer that's in my
    heart.
It sings praise to the Lord for this
    new start.

1988

Jehová Reina

Jehová reina con alegría.

Jehová es el triunfador.

El nos aparta de cuanta espina

haiga a nuestro alrededor.

3 de febrero del 1988 – Florida

Con Cristo Viviré

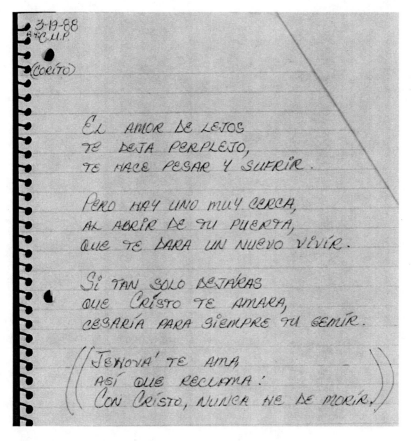

3-19-88
8ª C.U.P.

(coríto)

EL AMOR DE LEJOS
TE DEJA PERPLEJO,
TE HACE PESAR Y SUFRIR.

PERO HAY UNO MUY CERCA,
AL ABRIR DE TU PUERTA,
QUE TE DARA UN NUEVO VIVIR.

SI TAN SOLO DEJARAS
QUE CRISTO TE AMARA,
CESARIA PARA SIEMPRE TU GEMIR.

(JEHOVA' TE AMA
ASÍ QUE RECLAMA:
CON CRISTO, NUNCA HE DE MORIR.)

19 de marzo del 1988

Te Seguiré, Te Serviré

No quiero tardar en seguirte
No quiero tardar en servirte

Porque si tan solo te siguiera, a Ti,
harás el mundo bello para mí.

Oh, Aleluya
Te voy a seguir
Oh, Aleluya
Te voy a servir

Porque contigo quiero vivir
Con Jesús Cristo quiero vivir.

16 de abril del 1988

Baby Love

Baby Love, I love you so
Tell me that you'll never go.
Your kisses, they're so sweet, their touch.
I love you babe, but maybe just too much.

Your smile just turns me inside out.
You never give me reason to doubt.
Baby Love, I love you so;
tell me that you'll never go.

Your sweet caress I can't resist;
I never knew this could exist.
You give me joy, you give me bliss.
Come, please give me one more kiss.

Angel eyes, please tell no lies.
Take me to the highest skies.
Together, baby, we can rise.

You make me come alive, so new.
If ever there's a love, it's you.
Baby Love, I love you, oh
So tell me you won't ever go.

Angel eyes,
just can't disguise!
I feel for you,
you know it's true!

Angel baby,
drive me crazy. . .
Love you so,
don't ever go. . .

Baby Love. . .
Angel Love. . .
I'm in heaven above.

Spring 1988

I COULD

IF I COULD, I WOULD;

KNOW THAT I SHOULD.

IF I DO, IT'S TRUE;

ONLY FOR YOU.

IF I STAY, FOR A DAY,

I'LL NEVER GO AWAY.

I SHALL GO, I KNOW,

AND MY TEARS OVERFLOW.

SO I LEAVE, I BELIEVE,

FOREVER TO GRIEVE.

June 1988

"RUNAWAY"

I could run away with you today
and leave all my troubles here to stay.
I could try to reach that distant star
by running away with you somewhere far.
And, oh, what an adventure we would share,
no one would follow us anywhere.

No one could stop us from having our fun;
no one could keep us from being as one.
I'd love to run away with you someday
and just leave all my fears to melt away.
I long for you to drive me away in your car;
who knows where we'll go or how far?

Living a fantasy, that's what it would be.
Taking a chance to finally be free!
In dreams, I'm hearing these words spoken,
and at night I sleep with my curtains open;
hoping that maybe you will appear,
and take me far away from here.

I could run away with you today
and leave all my troubles here to stay.
I could try to reach that distant star
by running away with you somewhere far.
And, oh, what an adventure we would share;
no one could stop us 'cause we wouldn't care.

Summer 1988

Yea Yea

Yea, Yea, say Save
Hey, Hey, be Brave
You know we're all the same
When we're playing the game
In this life of pain
Someone must remain
Yea, Yea, say Save
Hey, Hey, be Brave.
There's no time to weep
When you're in so deep
Pieces come unglued

Don't let yourself be fooled

July 1988

Time to Grow

There comes a time when you
        begin to grow,
When more and more each day
        you need to know
How it feels to live outside of
        ~~the~~ four walls;
Outside, the voice of life is
        crying its calls.
The time is fast approaching
        don't be afraid to fall.
If you want to find yourself,
        then give it your all.
Listen to the fears of others
        and you'll remain a child.
Try to do what everyone wants,
        it'll only drive you wild.
Just gather your dreams together,
        get up and go.
The time for it is now, 'cause
        this is your show.

July 1988

Whispering Wind

He was just a fantasy,
A dream come true, not real:
The fairy tale of a love
I'll never be able to feel.

Perhaps it's all just a wish
For something out of reach;
A lesson I have yet to learn,
But somehow I must teach.

I've never known what love is,
Unless it's the endless pain
Of tears brought on by sorrow
That on my pillows remain.

Love's said to be like magic,
Fulfilling one's life's desire,
(I was told some time ago
By a gallantly charming liar).

The whispers of the lonely wind
Are the only comfort I've found
On those nights I lie awake, wandering,
Through my world of a merry-go-round.

August 1988

Thoughts of a Learned Novice

Thoughts of a learned novice:
    Was there ever a spoken promise?
[An unspoken YES.]
...just a wrong guess!
    No,...not a word...
But something
    ...was heard:
(More like a feeling)
Did you see me kneeling ???

Two that must part:
        Numbness of the heart --
A heart that's left pleading;
See her eyes bleeding.
Red: "the colour of my soul".
Unspeakable emotion takes its toll.

Tasting the salt of my fear,
    You claim that tears are clear.

Morsels of lust end in waste;
Never beg a beggar for a taste.
I still have tomorrow.
    What do you know of my sorrow?

Bitterness shall and will remain...
...Don't forget about the pain.

September 27, 1988

Diciembre 3, 1989

" Que Quiere La Bella?"

Cuando en la noche se esfuma una estrella,
tambien se derrama una lagrima.
Brillan las demas estrellas, como tambien
.   brillan sus ojos -- Son los ojos de Ella.
¿Que quiere La Bella?

Pero no llora por lo desvanecido,
ni por lo que ha suffido.
Tampoco llora por alegría,
pues por dentro se siente fría.
Necesita el calor de un cuerpo amado,
pero el que la arropa y duerme a su lado
No es el con quien sueña despierta
Ni con el quien sueña de siesta.

Sus sueños la confunden, pues no tienen sentido.
Y todo lo que siente se vuelve un laberinto.
Caen mas estrellas dejando hueyas
Y el cielo llora junto con ella
¿Que quiere La Bella?

CARD GAME

Mother sits across from her daughter,
holding in her hand her last card.
And if you asked her how to play
She'd tell you it's not so hard.
"My love," she'd say, "Just keep a straight face,
even if you've lost your last ace."

Well, her daughter plays on, she knows the game.
She's seen it played time and time again.
She's played it often enough to know
that it takes more than one to end a show.

Dear mother, where has that soft look gone?
There are no smiles, no smile, not a trace.
What could happen to grieve you for so long?
Harsh lines surround your saddened face.

And Daddy comes home, he greets the dog,
then he wearily sits down to eat.
He moans and groans, then says hello,
all this while rubbing his feet.

"Play on, dear child," mother says,
"Let's see how this hand'll end,"
as she looks away then down at her card,
and wishes she could just pretend.

Such hard work he labored in vain
If only to live up to the family name.
All mother ever needed was the love for a wife,
Given to her only, for the rest of her life.

December 1989

Pearl

What is it you hold so dear as a Pearl?
What is it you hold so dear in this world?
Don't you know...

What is it you hold so dear as a Pearl?
What is it you hold so dear in this world?
Don't you know...

And if you had a Pearl,
Would you name it a Girl?
And if you had a Girl,
Would you give her the world?
Don't you know in this world....

Everything is temporal.
Everything is temporal.
Everything is temporal.
Don't you know...

Find your Pearl, and make it right for you.

Circa 1990 - Chicago, IL

Sin Reproches

No te reprocho nada de lo que hemos vivido;

No te reprocho nada de lo que yo he sufrido

Porque yo vivo enamorada del sueño que me diste, mi ilusión.

Y es que me tienes enredada, tus besos me atan a tu corazón.

Yo te confieso, a veces pense que te habías ido.

Y te confieso, noches pasada en vela me han herido.

Pero al mirarte a tu cara se borra toda duda, suspición.

Tu amor se nota a clara, y olvido toda duda, confusión.

Y es que yo vivo enamorada del ardor que en tus brazos siento.

Y es como si al querer volara; asi me hace sentir tu gran amor.

No me reproches, si a veces sueles verme en silencio.

Piensa en las noches, las noches en las que yo siempre pienso.

Porque yo vivo enamorada, del sueño que me diste, mi ilusión.

Y es que me tienes enredada; tus besos me atan a tu corazón.

24 de febrero del 1990

FINDING GOLD

July 24, 1990
Seems like I can't get out of this state of poverty
    that persists in hanging around.
Everytime I think my flight is assured, I'm driven
    another foot underground.
Sometimes I feel I'm over six feet under already
    and just can't rest in peace.
This life that I'm living is nothing but hardship
    and I can't get any relief.
Perhaps if I had someone by my side to share the
    load with me day by day.
Perhaps if I had someone to wake up to instead of
    just a memory.
Perhaps if I struck it rich, discovered my pot of gold,
    or was appreciated by my boss.
Perhaps if I had no bills, no stress, some peace of mind,
    I wouldn't feel this loss.
Perhaps, maybe just perhaps . . . I just keep dreaming
    of this brighter tomorrow.
I keep hoping for something wonderful to happen to
    end all of my sorrow.
I'm trying to make it happen, working hard trying
    to get ahead, and being true.
I'm a friend for those who need me, but sometimes
    too supportive, to you.
So busy caring 'bout your needs, never place mine
    in the place they belong.
Always feel I've never done enough or that I'm
    doing something wrong.
How could I let myself get so lost; I'm drowing
    in a pit of abandonment.
I've got to take control of my future, but I don't
    know if I can handle it.
Well, I'm going to try anyway, 'cause I've only got one me.
And if leaving is what it takes, then it's gonna have to be.
I'm so tired of struggling, and alone I'll struggle
    for a while, I know.
But knowing that one day I will be free gives me
    strength enough to go.
I have to reach for those dreams before I get too old.
Because just dreaming of what I want won't help me find my gold.
My gold is a happy life, and of my lover, to be his wife.
My gold is security, a house that's a home:
All the things in life I should have of my own.
And love is the greatest gold of them all.
Money just helps me survive if I should ever fall.
Gotta try for those dreams I've kept for so long.
Gonna try for a new answer that this time won't be wrong.
So goodbye cheap labor, hello educator.
Goodbye credit debtor, hello bank ~~lender.~~ teller.
Goodbye shoes for walking, hello all-day parking.
Goodbye singing blues, hello happy tunes.
My life is starting over, leaving behind my past mistakes
And this time I'm going to make it, no matter what it takes!

Haunting Memories

You brought me to the peak of desire.
You stole my heart and then set it on fire.
You brought me to the highest elevation.
And now I've come to this revelation:

There will always be a place in my heart for you,
Because the love that I felt for you was true.
And although you left me brokenhearted,
With eyes full of tears as we parted,
I can't hold your request for freedom against you.
If you had to be free, then what else could I do.

But everytime I see a smile like yours, my heart aches.
I've tried to forget, but I don't know what it takes.
Lovers have come and gone and I've stayed the same;
But something in me changes when I hear your name.

I let you go your own way when you asked,
Thinking I could just erase you from my past.
But your memory won't let me be;
So I guess I'll never be free.
At least one of us is free to love someone new.
In my heart I know, I'll always love you.

I just hope you're happy with your new choice.
And I hope she can erase the sound of my voice
I can remember your words of love to me:
Made me so blind that I just couldn't see.
As for me, I don't think I can ever trust again
In promises of a love that will never end.
I believed in your words because I believed in me and you.
But now I'm alone; you tell me what is really true.

You brought me to the highest elevation
And now I've come to this revelation:
That love breeds more than just a sensation;
It breeds loyalty, trust, and adoration.

Lovers have come and gone and more will come, I know.
But maybe, just maybe, one will come who'll never go.
And then I'll be able to say that I'm finally free
from the memory of your love that's haunting me.

July 25, 1990

"Silent Treatment" 11-10-90

Your Silence hurts more than anything
you could ever say against me.

I don't know which I'd rather do: speak
or leave... (convince me).

Don't want to leave you; it's not
that crucial.

But I can't say two words without
wanting to cry.

You speak maybe two words in
reply.

Maybe you feel I'm being cold.

I just want to hold you like I did
before.

Baby, this situation is gettin' kinda
old.

If you don't say a little something
more to me, I'll have to go.

I can't deal with silence, it's too
much the hurt it inflicts →

I can't deal with silence; I'd
    rather you had a fit.

Although I hate cheating, at least
    I know you care.

Because silence from you feels like
    you don't really care, (like I'm
not even there).
I wonder if you still love me...

I told you I still loved you.

If we can't talk to each other,
    how will either of us know.

If I go home, will you ask me not
    to go?

Silence, from you, hurts more
    than anything you could ever do.
        ...Speak to me...

November 10, 1990

Altamonte Springs, FL

January 5, 1991
"Tears for a Lullaby"

Can you feel my pain?
You say you're hurt inside.
But can you feel my pain?
A part of me has died.

You haven't seen my tears
that fall when I try to sleep at night.
You haven't felt the fears
that greet me with the morning light.

A faceless face without a name
sentenced to death without repree.
I look to my hands with disdain
For they've been bloodied by the life within me.

Forgiveness is all that I can ask
But I need more than that, I know.
To forgive is not an easy task.
And so I pray for my soul.

I already live in hell inside.
I already live in pain.
I already feel as if I'd died.
Tell me, can you feel my pain?

Love

Love as though
it were your
last day to live.
Live as though it were
your last day to Love.
Forever, ...If Love could be
then I'd want it to be
You.

July 2, 1991

Bathroom

A room that's bare
and everything's white
Except for your hair
with its curls so tight
Scattered everywhere
Brought to life by the light
A light bulb that's bare
and everything's white.
And you're still there
but now there's no light.

Realistically bare
Trying so hard to fight
The memory of this room where
I'd bathe each night

And where
I'd smile at your sight
and where
sometimes you'd hold me tight
and where
everything was white
except for your hair
curling so tight
scattered here and there
Now hidden in the night.

Realistically bare
this room seemed so bright
But I'm no longer there
And the memory I must fight

July 4, 1991 – Baton Rouge, LA

Living or Dreaming

12:20 am   7-6-91

(Are you really living,
Are you really alive.
Or are you living someone else's dream.)

Sometimes I wonder
if what I'm working so hard for
is it what I really want

Am I really living
or am I just walking in a dream
Someone else's dream.

How can I know?
I know because sometimes I'm
                    not Alive.
I'm just like a sleepwalker.

If I could feel what I'm living
Then maybe... just maybe.
But I'm only dreaming.

(The only time I feel alive is
when I'm with you.)   (cup)

July 6, 1991

Excuse Me

Thursday 12:30 a.m.   March 19, 1992

...Excuse me while I go into a corner and cry!

Why? I ask. Why? Why?

But I already know that many have suffered & struggled long before me! I should feel lucky or spared not to have shared their burdens.

Still, I ask why. Why?

...Excuse me while I go into my corner and cry!

Life seems like an unending struggle; just when you catch your breath you have to run again.

When do I get to stop & smell the roses? They'll be no more when I die. Only the ones thrown upon my casket.

March 19, 1992

Yugoslavia
(Sarajevo)

Flee the bloodshed.
Welcome not the pain.
Even though out of my family
only one remains.

A refugee in danger
Of becoming insane,
I peep through the bars that
keep me from the rain.

I am but a child…
I barely understand
This war that goes on between
the brotherhood of man.

July 21, 1992 – Baton Rouge, LA

*(Dedicated to a boy from Sarajevo
I saw in an AP wire wildshot,
sitting in a cage on the
back of a truck.)*

Soul, Sista

Sista, why do you stay?
I can kneel down on my knees
                    and pray
but all the wishin' in the world
    ain't gonna make him go away.

Sista, leave him today!
You can beg, plead, and pray,
but ain't nothing gonna change
                        his ways.

'Cause he was made that way,
    no not born that way.
And though he may say (I love you),
    it don't mean he'll stay.

Look at yourself, just wastin' away.
All those years, sista, why do you
                            stay?
Ain't no love so great that'll make
                            me say
I'ma sit 'n rot, give my soul away.

November 7, 1992

And we talked...

He reminisced about our good times
and skimmed over the bad times.

I listened...
I felt no tug at my heart over the memories;
I felt no pain inside over the lost chimes.

And he talked...
He said he wanted advice,
yet all he talked about was what we had before.

So I spoke...
I asked if this was all
he had wanted to talk to me for.

I knew his game
though he claimed it wasn't a ploy
I'd played it before,
but not this time, oh no, boy.

I listened, as he rambled,
But my heart could not feel,
and my mind was distant.
Still, I listened.

And when I left, he wondered
if I would sleep at peace
or think of all that was said.

But I'd thought long ago of more
and had left it long behind.
I slept fast and sound in my bed.

The nightmares that haunted me in the past
shall no longer chase my sleep away.

Let him reminisce all he wants...
I weep no longer, for I've seen the day.

He can talk and I may even talk back,
but as we talk, I know.

Life has set its course for me,
and I have somewhere to go.

His life is in his destiny;
mine is in my own.

Now I listen one last time
as he talks alone.

December 8, 1992 – Baton Rouge, LA

Seashells by the Sea

Childhood memories...
of pink sea shells in a wine jar.

They came from the shore
seen from "Maria Libertad."

My school was on one side of the highway,
la playa was on the other.

A labor of love is what it was
to linger for an hour or so,
before walking home.

The water was dirty,
but the shells were a beautiful, bright pink...
the color of my Dreams.

When I'd walk in the door,
Mami would be angry.
"¿Donde estabas?"

I wasn't supposed to walk home.

Me daban un limazo.
But it was worth it to have seen the red flowers
in the busy bushes along the sidewalk...

It was worth it, to bring home a treasure.

I had plans to cover a jewelry box with them
once the jar was filled.
But before I could reach the top of the jar,
death came.

My shells & "la playa" were lost in the move.

It's years later, and I still remember
those pretty shells...
One day I'll go back and look
for the shells Mom threw away.

And this time, death won't come.
And I'll stay.

[In memory of Puerto Rico, where I found my first seashell
on La Playa de Sabana Seca and lost mi Abuelita
(great grandma) and Pachin (grandma.)]
12-8-1992

Coco Loco

Yo no soy loca
Tu eres el loco

Tengo Cabeza
Y tu: tienes coco

Pero con coco
yo no voy

Porque, loco,
"loca" yo no soy…

Para pa-pa-para-pa-pa-pa-pa-PA!
Wooo Weee!
He-Pa…

Pero con Co-Cooo
Co-Coo!

(To the beat of 1-2, 1-2, 1-2, 1-2-3)

Winter 1992

I in Me

Thursday ————— February 25, 1993

I.
I am.
I am still.
I am still searching.
I am still searching for the
                    I in me.

Woman

I am a vessel that's
full of love,
full of patience & strength,
full of kindness & empathy,
compassion & savvy.

Be careful with this vessel, though.

If you try to drink
all that's within,
I will inevitably
run empty.

And then I will
have nothing but
hollowness left.

Remember, vessels
can be filled
when they're emptied.

But unlike a vessel,
this woman may not.

3-6-1993

"I Love You, Still" (By: Cynthia M. Portelatin)
Remember when I said I loved you?
Well, I love you, still.
Remember when I said I need you?
I still need you -- still.
The tingles have turned into a glow
This love is growing strong.
And this peace that dwells within me
Tells me it's with you I belong.
Remember when I said I love you?
Well, I love you, still.
And I'll tell you again and again,
Because I always will.

March 1993

Baton Rouge, LA

Phobias

4-23-93

(On all the "Phobias" used to excuse hate.)

Why is it that we judge ourselves the way we do
When all that matters is what we give, from "me to you?"
Why do differences fill our hearts with hate
Why can't we work toward the goal to which we all relate.
Love is universal, peace is desired by all
but by those who hunger for power, those who make the call.
No one will reach the Summit of happiness sought within
With prejudice and bigotry unacknowledged as our sin.

By Cynthia M. Portalatín
Baton Rouge, LA

Was There Love

Passion is a fleeting feeling.
But love can last forever,
if nurtured.
Like a fireworks show,
passion sparks awe.
But where is the feeling
after the lights fade away?
The beauty of a reoccurring
sunrise or sunset
never ceases to amaze me... The
Love given day to day by
you is the same.
After the passion, after the
sparks have faded, what
matters then is:
was there love?
Without love, nothing remains.
But with love, the sunrise
will come... forever.

June 13, 1993

Sit Still Says the Lord

"Sit still" said the Lord,
as I fumbled, restless with indecision.
"Sit still and hear my word."
Still, I wavered; still, I fumbled.
Now I'm still, as I listen...
And there is peace, gone is confusion.
The peace of love and comfort keeps
me still.
Whatever life throws my way, I can
stand strong on the word.
The Lord leads me, comforts me and
keeps me... still.

August 29, 1993

Let Me Know

If you want me, let me know.
If you don't, then let me go.
But don't keep me waiting,
forever anticipating.
How much longer must I wait
on this love you contemplate
How much longer shall I wait for you
to know who you are.
Will you find yourself beside me
or will you end up very far.
I hunger for you, long for you
I'm thunder for you, strong for you
I'll wonder for you, was I wrong for you
'Cause love is being one in one
not split in two.
So let me wait no longer.
Either, help our love grow stronger
or let go.

'Cause baby if you want me
you've got to let it show
And if you don't know
by now, then you'll never
know.

November 8, 1993

75 *Bloom Forever ~ by Cynthia M. Lamb*

"OLAS DE AMOR"
I miss my love
like I once missed mi playa, mis caracoles.

But the tears are no longer those of a child.
They are now the ache of a woman's heart.

I miss my love,
like I missed playing in the arena, quemandome con el sol.

The gentle rocking of the waves at night
is no longer what my body needs to sleep.

Now, it is the waves felt in my love's arms that I miss,
Mis olas de amor.

The anger I felt toward the palm trees of the north,
which so betrayed those of my beloved Isla
is translated, transformed
from one love to another, more human to the touch.

And the sight of happy lovers together
deepens the wound I carry by choice

Because I cannot let go of this ache.

I cannot abandon the pain.

It will keep the memory of my love alive,
until I once more can relive my dream.

Or until las olas cubran mi alma.

By Cynthia M. Portalatin
Noviembre 17, 1993 p.m.
Richmond, Virginia

A Mother's Dreams

2/6/94

My mother lives her dreams
   through me.
Happy she is not, within.
Her life has been long-
   suffered.
But if she could live her
   dreams,
if time could begin anew
   and return her youth...
She'd be much like me.
   I'd like to think we
   would be the best of friends,
   Though we are now as
   mother & daughter.
Her life was stolen by the
   demands of all our lives.
Her dreams were put aside,
   buried, so that we may
   perhaps fulfill ours.
My dream now is no longer of
   fortune & fame.

My dream now is of peace
for her soul...&
of happiness: to see it
in her eyes & smile.
I grieve for her losses &
would gladly carry her pain
if it would grant her at
least one day of rest.
My mother's dreams are my
own: two simple truths
we seek — peace & love

CMP

2/6/94
5:30 p.m.
Richmond, VA

Looking for me?

Oh I can't be this no mor', can't be this no mor'
Got to find the me that I've bin lookin' for.

Oh I can't be this no mor', can't be this no mor'.
Got to find the me that I've bin lookin' for.

I've got to find the me
I can't be this no mor'.

I need music and flowers and paint and serenity
I need time to explore my own identity.

My hours go by given to someone else
And I've lost sight of myself.

I wanna come home to me
Not this tired old person I've come to be

I want to feel alive, I want to look forward to each day
I want to feel the wonder and awe of beauty and discovery

Where am I? Where am I?

My bank account is still empty, and my car doesn't have
enough gas
to take me where I really want to go.

Yet I'm working every day and supposedly making money.
Who's got my money?
The same people who took my fears and fed me lies.

Give me my fears, and let them wake me out of the slumber
I've lingered in for too long.

'Cause I can't go on...
I've gotta find the me in me I've bin wantin' to be for so long.

March 2, 1994 – Richmond, VA

Richmond

(Composed 6·25·94) · (while driving to the airport)

Living here in Richmond

Ain't nobody rich, man

'Kept the politician

Living for division,

'Kept the "boss-man"

Livin in Peach-Land.

But no—never the Brother-man

Who stretches out this bleedin' hand.

June 25, 1994

It's a Shame

They say "it's a shame you only go out alone."
And I agree, but it's just the way I want it to be.
"You won't be alone for long," they say
And I know it could be true.
But 'makes no difference what they say
'Cause all I want is you.
I see fine men, but they don't see me
Or could it be I pretend
Not to notice if they look at me or stare
Because I don't want to end
This feeling I feel for you; I'm trying to hold on
But it's getting harder and harder to hold on.

Baby, honey, can't you see I love you,
And it hurts so bad inside
You say you love me but you're still
Not ready for me to be your bride.
I've stood waiting for years, waiting
for you to take my hand.
"Take my hand and walk with me
Along the beach, we'll trace our
Names in the sand.
We'll kiss 'from here until eternity'
We'll love each other endlessly.
We'll build sand castles and
Listen to our dreams through seashells
As the salt water cures our fears."

But you don't hear me, though you say you do.
You're just a boy whose fears echo
in the wind that drowns out my love for you.
And it's no wonder when you say you love me
I no longer feel warm inside like
when you used to hold me.
I keep my pillow close to me at night,
and wish it were you instead
I'm trying to hold on, but feel like
I'm gonna wake up dead.
One day I'll wake up "dead to your voice,"
dead to your love
And I won't have a choice...
But to go out alone.
"It's a shame, they say, I know it's true.
Holding up my world for you.

July 19, 1994

Wrong Timing

A meeting of the minds,
she said . . .

I'd had a taste once,
but was too young
to know to let go
and let it be
whatever it was to be.

This time, I'll be cool.

There is no "right thing to say."
There is only thought
and thoughts are spoken
visions are shared

We taste each other's fatasies
But we're not talking sex

A momentary glimpse . . .
I liked what I saw.
Was he being honest?
It didn't matter; but it does.

We connected.
Now, I understand . . .
But our timing is all wrong.
Maybe in another life
we will connect
and the timing will be right.
Maybe . . .
And when this time comes again,
all will be right.

August 9, 1994 – Norfolk, VA

This Moment

We have this moment
And even though
we did not dance
This moment is ours
Be it a distant memory . . .
Never mind if you should forget.
I think not on our sorrow
but only this moment

Perhaps I am selfish . . .
That may be so.
What would you call this?

I wonder why you're here.
You say you love her
And would never leave her
Yet we share these thoughts
And we share our trust.

Still, we did not dance.

Perhaps that was best.
I think of you and smile
And know that if only . . .

for a moment . . . . . .

for a moment . . .

that moment . . .

I could dream

Yes, I could dream.

August 12, 1994 - Richmond, VA

Say I Do

August 12, 1994 -- 9 something p.m. #2
Richmond, VA -- By C.M.P.

Why lovers who thought they'd love forever
Say "I do,"
And then don't . . .
I don't understand

I crave what they've thrown away
But perhaps I am the lucky one
For when my heart is broken
When my heart is broken
There are no legal fees
there are no ties that bind
There are only goodbyes
And my heart is free to bleed, then heal . . .
Then love again.

And yet I crave
what they run away from.
They too must have craved like I
Am I better off alone?

I no longer search
Yet my soul,
my soul is still longing . . .

Perhaps someday I'll understand
But I keep hoping
And I keep dreaming
That one day
One day . . .
I'll know the joy of "forever"
And that Forever will be my joy.

One Day

August 12, 1994 -- 9 something p.m. #3
Richmond, VA -- By C.M.P.

I have loved for so long
Different men have come and gone

I have given my all
And everytime I take the fall

I feel that here I shall always lay
Broken hearted, but I never stay

I may vow
I may vow

But I always get back up again somehow

On and on . . .
On and on . . .

(One day . . . One day . . .)
        We'll walk hand in hand
        to "never-never land"

        It must be called that for a reason
        Maybe because it's out of reach

        But I'll never say never
        I'll never say never

And I'll dream . . .
I'll dream on and on

And my dreams will keep me alive
Until I can live my dream

Burned

By CMP
8·18·94
10:47 p.m

We made a pact,
and I've kept my word, true
But now you're back,
And my thoughts once again turn to you.

How calm I was to see you again.
But to me you spoke, I could not pretend
Not to notice your touch, the warmth of your smile
My quickening pulse begged you to stay for a while.

You're such a charmer, so I stayed away
But now you call me; you want to play.

You say you're braver now
What changed your mind?
You said you'd cheat never—
Those words were so kind...

I tried to keep my part of the deal,
But here you come again
Making the feeling all too real
And soon I won't want it to end.

I'm playing with fire
by yielding this desire

But I won't get burned as long as I remember
No matter how good it feels, it can't last forever.

August 18, 1994

The Dream

You kiss me
I can't hold back
Remember now,
we made a pact
To never come
so close again
Unless we saw
it through the end

Our pact we've kept,
but closer still
draw to the fire
against our will
Ignore the guilt
drown in the feel
Fed by your touch
My eyes appeal

Reach for me,
lend me your kiss
Let me believe
it's me you miss
Be it wrong
it all feels right
Wonderful . . .
Just for tonight.

For you to stay
would be my wish
But play content
--Temporary bliss
Know it is all
to never ask . . .
The future promises
No Love to last.

Your life's been made
Mine, just begun
And I know that when
all's said and done
I'll find comfort
Memories: caress
Bring a smile
. . . nothing less.

Open your soul
Live what you feel
For this moment in time
The dream is real

August 24, 1994 - Richmond, VA

AJP

Met you at the right time
When I needed a friend
But when I see your eyes shine
I can't deny nor pretend.

Memories of a younger love
Come swimming into view
And I hear their echoes
As I think of you.

Your smile is like a breath of fresh air
Who knew you'd smile my way?
But I'm still tied to another
So I can't ask you to stay.

See, all I needed was a friend
To keep me company
And I enjoy your conversation
But that's all it can be.

I love my man, despite his faults
And even though he's far
He's closer to me in my heart
Than you to me are.

But I like you; Yes I do.
You're as sweet as they come
Though for me you're not the one.

I said you came at the right time
But maybe it's the wrong time
For so long I'd been doin' time
Thought I was just wastin' my time.

Wastin' my time...
On a love who was drifting away
And now he says he wants to stay.

But I'd been drifting too
Now I'm drifting straight to you...
The wind has caught my sails and I
Feel soon we'll have to say goodbye.

I'll remember you my friend
Your smile brightened up my days
When I thought the rain would never end.
You brought me better days.

With this one wish I leave you:
This I hope you find
Someone to love & keep who knows
You're one of a kind.

August 31, 1994

Fabrizzio

You came into my life

Like a warm, soft summer breeze

But now your love is strong

Like the winds that sweep the ocean's waves.

In my heart, the waves crest
    and fall like thunder.

And I admit sometimes I'm afraid.

But each day I face my fear I discover

A new wonder in your arms,

A new smile in your eyes, and...

A braver love than I have ever known.

Chance let us meet, and choice made us friends

But love will keep us together...

                If we believe.

9:00pm, September 26, 1994

Paper Dreams

Paper dreams
are now
reality.

Love: a simple
fantasy...

Now I see
my dreams
are real.

You are every—
(thing)
I feel.

CML 10-1-94 10:20 pm

"Ticho"

He's as sweet as vanilla icecream
  on a hot summer's day.
He's as spicy as jambalaya
  on a Bayou breezeway.
He's as cool as the soothing waters
  of a river's flow.
Come to give me a cool drink
  to soothe my tired soul.
He's as warm as a summer breeze,
And can be such a tease...
"Cool aid" to quench my thirst
Mmm, he tastes better than the
                              first!

I'm happy once again.
...And Love is Beautiful.

October 1994 – Richmond, VA

Hardened

You were right, Ticho.
I was wrong, dicho.
You said you'd right, mijo
But you took too 'long, mijo

You were correct: I don't know
    How to Love
I was definately wrong, and now
    I keep praying to my God Above

That He may teach me how to love
    the Right way, the Only way.

I thought Love meant long suffering.
    Because I spent 4 long years
                        waiting.

I thought Love meant loyalty.
Because I was faithful to the "T."

But my "Ex," though faithful to me, too,
Never wanted to marry me.
Or perhaps he was ready last September
But that's when I met you, remember.

And I was too quick to run with your Love.
And I lost sight of a Higher Love.

Now I'm paying the price for my sins.
Prayer is how I make it through my days.
He who sins never wins.
Or so "they" say.

You don't hate me but your eyes are cold.
And you don't see my soul is old.
I've loved so many different men.
Will never make this error again.

But now I understand "I swear."
(A song I hated before meeting you.)
Because I see you really do care.
I listened too late to know it was true.

I threw away your ♥ w/a careless
        whisper on my part.

Would you ever forgive my stupidity?
Would you ever forgive my nudity?

Perhaps, but now there's not much left
        to say.
'Cause your heart has hardened and you'll
        go your own way ...

                                    CML
                                    5:40 am

October 22, 1994

WAFFLE HOUSE FRIEND

Charlotte, N.C. ~ 4.50 a.m.
(Somewhere on I-85)

Met a kind Spirit tonight.
The "Waffle House" was the only
place in sight. I asked the
Lord, my God, to show me the
way. So that I may never
go astray. But I ended up in
this warm place. And felt
at home when I saw her face.
If I'm ever back this way
again, I'll have a new
friend until the End. ~

November 6, 1994

Hawk

Predator, you stalk my love...
Prey – I give in to your caress
Thinking not of The One Above
Letting you take of me My Best
To love the way you do
Think I could; so do you

A heart claimed by another
Got my soul; met my mother
Must apologize, put out the fire
That burned us both in desire

Could love you just as much
Every time I feel your touch
Left to dream of cloud-filled skies
Never want to hear goodbyes

November 9, 1994 – Richmond, VA

Angel

Nov. 14, 1994
(en route to Georgia)

Angel,
I clipped your wings & heard your cry.
But they'll grow again & soon you'll fly.

Because of me your love has died.
And so I'll try to explain the why.

I try to mend your broken dream
But all you hear is my silent scream.

I never gave up my dream, my love.
And I've 'surrendered' it all to the Lord above.

If Thou shall deem me worthy of a love anew,
I promise he will have a heart like you.

And I shall never leave his side again.
'Till death do us part — until the end.

We'll work together, side by side.
Crossing creeks and streams that are rivers wide.

To spread God's grace, love & joy
And teach every little girl & boy
That through Christ Jesus all are saved
For the road he traveled, with gold is paved

Car of My Dreams

Man of beautiful eyes.
Sold me a pretty lie!
The car of my dreams
Can't begin to hide my screams.
But I'll settle for this black beauty
Till I can set my spirit free.
'Cause to find a lover who's just like me
Would hurt my chest
cut too deep.
No longer searching.
I let my job move me now.
Educate and relate.
Can anybody appreciate the love a young
                            woman has to offer?

Nov. 14, 1994
10:39 pm (Amy)

Morning

Wooly hair and a heartbeat
To melt away a *supple* heartweak
Skin smooth *as ice* as a snake's
Too loved and awaits *is much*
                    a touch.

March 19, 1995

The War Within

There's a war brewing
inside most hearts today.
The bitterness of hurts
gone too long unnoticed
is churning its sour milk.
It's curdling within.
We war with ourselves.
Destroy ourselves.
And I don't even know
if Love is the answer
anymore.
Don't even know if Love can
be enough for a man to
stop the hate or for a woman
to heal.
I used to write love songs to
heal my soul.
Bitterness has joined fear
and chained my hand to the
world. And the lyrics
aren't so free anymore.
The only hope left is
in my song.

April 19, 1995 – Athens, GA

101   *Bloom Forever* ~ by Cynthia M. Lamb

Bus Depot Dream

Bus depot dream
Chocolate supreme

Eyes speak tenderness
So gently you caress

My weary dreams
My unheard screams

Kisses that could melt
The loneliness I've felt

"I'm not easy," I said
Praying my eyes you'd read

Your smile was sweet
As you rubbed my feet

Day turned to night
We promised to write

Then you rode to Texas' sun
I wondered if you'd be the one

To send for me, to live for me
To love with me, for eternity

Dreaming, I met the Bayou sun
Coulda been nice to be the one

To come to you
To love with you

Though sun's rise and set
I said I would not forget

And when the lonelies get me blue
I close my eyes and think of you

You are chocolate supreme
My bus depot dream

April 1995

Bloom Forever ~ by Cynthia M. Lamb 102

FEAR

I took a chance coming here
I went against my deepest fear

I left behind the dreams I cherish
For fear that alone I would perish

I forge ahead still unsure
If this heart will ever cure

Don't want to open up again
Won't even reach out to a friend

I know I can't continue to hide
Behind this wall of foolish pride

But many lurk outside in wait
...snatch my words, turn them to hate

So I say little and listen more
Knowing I can't walk out the door

I can't leave until I'm ready
And though my sigh is getting heavy

It won't be long before I know
The time is right for me to go

Will you come with me – do you dare
To close your eyes and let go of despair

To taste the sweetness of freedom
You must let go of false kingdoms

Grab hold of your fear, look it in the eye
Make a wish, and kiss that fear goodbye

Take a stand for what you believe is true
Or someone else will define the "I" in you.

April 23, 1995

Living

Living should be free & easy
Our laughter, light & breezy
Taking care to feed the soul
With love essential to the whole
The whole meaning all of you
But he and she and they, too
For joy shared is reflected again
In the laughter of a friend.

4/25/95 cmp
Jackson, MS

Queasy Feeling

Feeling strange today
Got a "queasy," nervous feeling
Like I've lost my balance
And I don't know how to regain my sense of self
As I was before I left you.
Have I lost myself?
Have I lost my will?
I don't know how to feel.
Nor do I know why I feel this way.
This "queasy," nervous feeling.
I'm not in control.
I live day by day with no major goals.
Afraid that what little control I have
will be lost if I stay with you.
But I want to stay.
For you care. Thanks to you I'm alive.
Will you help me sleep through the night?

June 9, 1995

In Love

February 14, 1996

👁 think ♡ is near...
When he whispers in my ear.
Rivers of pleasure flow deep within
Uncovered only by the warmth of your skin
Beneath the masks of coolness & pride
Ever lies a love as strong as the tide
Nothing compares to what we feel inside

14 de febrero del 1996 – Athens, GA

Enamorada

Pensando en tí estuve cuando me vistes
Al parecer ya te conocía, y lo supistes
Porque esa noche de la mano me cogiste
Y desde entonces ya no me siento triste

Nunca pense que hoy estaríamos enamorados
Nunca soñe que amaneceríamos abrazados

Que bonita es la vida
Cuando nos sorprende con la alegría
De un inesperado encuentro
Que nos llega como el viento

Me despiertas de un sueño profundo
Para compartir un nuevo mundo
Lleno de la esperanza y de la ilusión
Que solo nos puede traer el amor

Febrero del 1996 – Athens, GA
(For RV)

Viento de Amor

En mi alma siento sollozar el latido de mi corazón.
  Mi corazón se ahoga en la tristeza que envuelve mi ser.

No entiende porque no está mi más dulce posesión.
  Y siento un vacío al no poder estar con mí querer.

Mi amor, cuanto te extraño, cuanto deseo...
  Estar contigo de nuevo y decirte "Te Quiero"

Invento excusas para llamarte, porque ansío...
  Sentir que me abraces, me beses – es mi anhelo.

Amor, tus palabras dulces, tu mirada, me hacen falta.
  Y por más que trate no me conformo con solo recordarte.

Miro tus fotos, y quisiera gritarle al viento en voz alta,
  "¡Necesito oírte, sentirte, abrasarte, y mirarte!"

Ojala al sentir el viento en tu cara, mires al sol,
  Y sientas el calor que mi amor te dejo...

Ríos de lágrimas que la distancia nos mando
  Abrirán un camino de rosas regadas de amor.

14 de noviembre del 1996 – Athens, GA
(for RV)

Poema Para Vivir

Hoy conocí una
    alma gemela
una alma como
    la mía

La conocí de día
    y mas de noche
cuando resplandia.

Como es posible
    que haya sufrido
    los mismos
    desengaños que
a veces nos juega
    la vida.

    Y sueño despierta,
y despierto en un
sueño. El espejo
me sonríe.

Y el gemelo me
    refleja la vida
de mi vivir.

Y es que todavía
no he vivido
mi destino. Pero,
la he de un día
vivir.

12 de agosto del 2000
Pasado de las 2:00 a.m.
San Juan, Puerto Rico

Worn and Loved

Today I feel worn
    like a favorite
    coat of leather
Like a favorite pair
    of shoes.

Some days I feel broken
    and then others I feel
    new.

And Dahlia is now three
And reminds me more of me.

Today I felt loved
    like a favorite
    teddy bear
That's worn & torn
    but is so dear.

Some days I want to be
    new, and then others
    ... just want to be true

And was I once three, too?

July 9, 2001 – Athens, GA

Early morning ramblings

My mind won't quit, and I'm up way too late again.
I'm dreaming in live color and waiting on this song to end.
Keep thinking I'll turn in, and then I listen in again
now here I am with an early morning rambling...

Will I ever find my perfect match, or a lasting love?
The book I read tells of 8 keys but none come from above
See Jesus was the only one who died for me
All the others ever did was lie to me
And now I see it all too clear
that all I ever thought was dear
was nothing but confusion
drowning in my illusion

Tears no longer cloud my sight
No longer do I have to fight
the emptiness, the loneliness,
the never-ending nothingness
He loved me first, now I love him
So great His love, He cleansed my sin

'Cause my heart's healed
my faith revealed
I'm finding out what's really real
is that my heart cannot conceal
that He who bore the greatest thorn
gave it all so I might be reborn

He loved me first, now I love him
So great His love, He cleansed my sin

5:12 AM , January 14, 2006

The Flame

Tonight an old flame called to say goodbye... again.
As if the first time he left I hadn't wondered if he'd died.
This time he said he just might disappear.
What was I supposed to feel?
The last time he disappeared I was left
wearing a ring full of hearts and many phone calls unreturned...
a wedding proposal w/o a date...
memories to break my heart every time.
So excuse me if this time I wasn't crying, and if this time
I didn't offer a safe haven.

No longer will I be the "paño de lagrimas" for a man's fears,
nor easily excuse a man's lies as though they were unintentional.
To me, actions speak louder than anything one can say,
even if the person is screaming.
Words are so powerful, but what you do or don't do
determines your fate in life.
That old flame flickered out on its own of his own doing,
and because he chose it.
I wonder how much time is time enough to heal such a deep wound.
I guess I'll have to wait and see.

My flame is still alive, though many have tried to put it out.
My flame is fed by God's undying love for me.
If God can love me when others couldn't, or wouldn't,
then I could also love me.
And so I will. And I am thankful that I can.

4:30 AM, Saturday, August 26, 2006
(for WPB)

Waiting...

In the darkness of the night
When I cry out,
"JESUS! How long must I wait?!"
When I cry out,
"FATHER! Haven't I been faithful and good long enough?!"
When I desperately seek answers from the Living Word,
and when my tears run like raging rivers...
My God tells me
"Wait...
"Not yet my child...
"Not here in this place...
"Wait....
"For I will restore you."
But I am lonely,
and I long for the promises my Lord said He'd grant me.
Like a child I stumble and weep when I've fallen.
My Father, full of grace and love, mercifully heals my wounds;
so that I may walk again in love and faith.
And so I wait.
Carried by His grace.
Protected by His love.
Inspired by His hope.
At peace with His will.
Moved by the Holy Spirit.
... my spirit claims His Victory.

March 3, 2007 – High Springs, FL

A Prayer for Strength

Father I ask for your guidance
as I walk this lonely
road in seeking purity
of mind, body and soul.

It is all too easy to fall into
the easiness of blaming my
fall into sin on simple
human frailty.

Give me strength to hold tight
to my moral values, and the
wisdom not to be seduced by
the lies spoken from foolish lips.

Let me be able to discern the true
spirit of those who would befriend
me for unclean purposes. Let me
not be confounded by their reasoning,
for their ways are deceiving.
Lead me down the path of righteousness.

Surround me with people who have
a heart to do your will and to live
a holy life – set apart from iniquity.
Bring me to a place where
good triumphs over evil. Where
truth is honored. Where love reigns.
So that I might indeed live on earth
as it is in heaven.

April 16, 2007 – High Springs, FL

$\wedge$

The Kiln

Rejoice in the knowledge

that just as clay burns in

a fiery kiln to emerge

a gloriously beautiful

porcelain vessel...

As we are God's creation,

when we go through the fire

of trials and tribulations,

we are cleansed and refined...

so we may emerge brilliant,

glorious & beautiful

...ready to receive

God's blessings.

11:40 AM, April 19, 2007 – Gainesville, FL

Bloom Forever ~ by Cynthia M. Lamb

High Tide, New Horizon

New job on the horizon...
They want me to practically walk on water.
...but I'm not Jesus...
Thankfully, my Jesus walks with me,
and He hears my prayers.
So I walk in faith, and dip my toes... in the water.
The water is cold, and the waves are strong
as they crash into the eastern shore of Maryland
on this balmy evening in late September.
The tide has risen.
The wind is fierce and loud,
but I can still hear screams of laughter from a group
running recklessly toward the rising waves.
Now that it is night, the ocean seems a dark, vast,
never-ending universe ahead.
Must not let fear keep me from looking ahead...
this, too, is God's creation.
The wind almost carries me across the sand
as I step back... jeans soaked, cheeks dry.
I can do this, I say to myself as I retreat from
welcoming the Atlantic.
I can do all things through Christ who strengthens me.
I walk on, ushered by the strong wind,
as if His wings were carrying me...
and I know I'm safe. I am loved. I am in His favor.
I can see the new Horizon...
It is Hope.

8:23 PM, Friday, September 21, 2007 – Maryland

Bloom Forever ~ by Cynthia M. Lamb   116

Lies

He lies with ease
uses words to tease

He spun a web
and filled my head

with fairytales I wanted to believe
but his words only meant to deceive

I should know better by now
I have lived too long to allow

Some guy to come along
and sing me a crazy song

But my heart is broken and I long
for arms to hold me that are strong

for whispers meant for my ears
for a tender touch to wipe my tears

I should have known it was all lies
when he'd never looked into my eyes

yet he professed a love forever
and said he would leave me never

I should have known it was too soon
but poetry made me dream with the moon

I should have paid attention to the signs
but instead I believed all the crafted lines

I know better; really I do
what sounds too good to be true

usually is just that, a lie
so I shouldn't even try

to believe in men whose words are lies
that eventually lead to sad goodbyes

God help me to believe again someday
but until then, here alone I'll stay.

12:40 AM, Saturday, December 1, 2007

117 Bloom Forever ~ by Cynthia M. Lamb

I Paint

I was careful to sand before I began.
Some of the wood was tough, despite the sanding.
Some of the paint continued to peel.
The sanding only made the railing look older.
Yet I sanded and smoothed out what I could.
I hammered a nail here and there to keep it sturdy.
I flicked away spider eggs and brushed off cobwebs.
I painted, and painted, and patiently painted.
I noticed mildew on the underside.
I rubbed away some and painted over the rest.
Would it come back? Perhaps, but not today.
I noticed deep cracks in the wood.
And I glopped on more paint.
I meant well. But I didn't have the right brush.
I painted, and painted, and lovingly painted.
My little sponge brushes didn't fare well.
They tore.
"Enough now," they pleaded.
But I would not be deterred.
My dog scratched at the door.
"Shhh! Shhh! Sit, Stay, No...!"
Neighbors pass and say hello.
I am thankful for the extra hour of sunlight.
Smile... chatter... splatter.
Never mind the cracks, the spots, the roughness.
It is in the painting that I am renewed.
My weathered rails are strong and new again.

Sunday, March 9, 2008 - High Springs, FL

ON THE EVE OF DAWN

traveling mercies in a carry-on
my mind wanders as I linger on
can't seem to get to bed tonight
looks like it's gonna be another long flight
where to this time, back again
look into the eyes of a friend
work to live, but live to see
when this life will set me free
I want to fly to another place
where I can bask in His grace
I want to be free from worry
seek to end this constant hurry
I want to float, as though I'm air
to be, to love, say I am where
I really wanna be...
this is where I wanna be
where I am gonna be
where I am totally free.

2:05 AM, Tuesday, August 5, 2008

Still

bring me to the still waters where I can rest my soul
bring me to the forgotten meadow where I can become
whole
my heart is weary, my tears have dried
there's no more need for me to hide
long ago I learned the game
somehow I forgot his name
where is my love the one I need
come to me with mighty speed
no, stay gone... time knows no wrong
and I'll remember what was our song
for I am broken when you're gone away
and here is where I'll plan to stay
don't want to venture out again
to find that someone I called friend
knew not who I was at all
so now I sit against my wall
and I write this lonely melody
that somehow keeps haunting me
give me solace, give me grace
return me to the human race.
I feel so gone, sometimes I'm falling ...
lost beneath the sounds of drowning
seagulls that were once as free
to roam above the mighty sea
oh how I long to feel the waves
to feel the arms of the one who saves
my tired heart, my tired soul
come quickly now... make me whole.

Friday, December 12, 2008

Caught

Of all the faces in the sea,
yours is the one I long to see.
The only one I aim to please...
I know those lips belong to me!
Your eyes so kind they warm my heart.
I just can't bear the thought of us apart.
You see above and beyond the wall
and let me know it's safe to fall
Into your arms where I long to be
Eyes closed, breathing in harmony.
I ache for your touch, I know your scent
I long for your kiss and moments spent
lying next to you, wrapped around you
enjoying you, intoxicated by you, too.
What am I going to do?
I'm caught, who knew?
I could write a thousand words about how I feel.
But none compare to the feeling that is so real
When you hold me close, and I melt and surrender
to a love you give freely -- so strong, yet so tender.
I won't even attempt to try to hide
This fire that burns deep inside
You quench my thirst, and you steady me
You've come to claim my heart for eternity.

February 5, 2009 – Tallahassee, FL
(for HS)

CLARITY

What I wouldn't give for some clarity

I'm surrounded by all this talk of disparity

So many ideas and not enough money

Dreaming of my land of milk and honey

Dreams bursting to be free

I'm afraid to test my destiny

I want to know but don't

I want to go but won't

I have to stay

Try to find my way

Work with what I've got in front of me

Mold my future, embrace my identity

Who am I but what I create

For God above to appreciate

So questions unanswered though they be

Spur me on toward finding the real me in me.

10:05pm, December 3, 2009

Change That I Need

Jan 2010

I sometimes don't like change.

I sometimes create change

I sometimes hate change

I sometimes need change

I sometimes fear change

I sometimes love change

I sometimes am changed;

because God changed me

I am learning to Be the

change that I need.

January 2010

Talking

What do I want to do?
I just want to talk with you
Sit with you for a while
And contemplate your smile
Your warmth invites me near
I love the way you lend me your ear
And when you share your heart
I feel mine warm wishing not to part

Old friend, you are new to me
Shared thoughts on who we both see
Reflected memories bouncing on the waves
As we discover how trust heals and saves...

Revealing a little at a time
As we slowly let the past unwind
Peeling back layers
Sending out prayers
I am understood again
In the presence of a true friend.

June 3, 2011 - 8:15pm
Tallahassee, Florida
(for LBL)

Chocolate Man

You are my knight in shining armor
... come to rescue me with your valor

I am in love, and my heart is full of glee
It is your undying love that set me free

I love you my Funny Valentine
Tell me that you'll always be mine

Sexy Chocolate Man, you make me hot
This Cinnamon Lady's sugar's surely got

A melting river of much desire
Beckons you to douse my fire

I give you of me my best
Not afraid to take the test

6:43 PM, Tuesday, July 5, 2011
(for LBL)

Love Birds

I am that bird set on autopilot...
I hear the call and fly into the wind
Dashing about, soaring with a few brave souls

Suddenly lifted up higher, I feel a shift in purpose...
No longer desiring to join formation
I break free to be swept higher still

Can my lungs breathe in the new air without bursting?

This joy I feel is uncontainable
As I burst into song and dive through the clouds
I can dance in the rain and dip my feet in the ocean
I can float in cotton clouds and bask in the glorious sun

When the moon arrives I realize I have lost all sense of time
And I am simply in this wondrous place
Where time means nothing and everything.

I now see your face reflected in my fallen tears

I look up to see you near, and I will you closer
Come closer my love, come closer
Together, we will fly, and it will all be worth it

Sweet journeys beckon us to new horizons
But for now we embrace in stillness...
And know our future is to sing together,
Dancing in unison, lifting our wings toward heaven.

We join hands and fly wherever God leads us.

I have found my purpose...

I am one with you.

8:39 AM, Friday, July 15, 2011
(for LBL)

Love, Infinity, and Beyond...

Whatever life gives us
for this I give thanks
sometimes life takes away
leaves us stranded on banks
of shores that are rocky
on seas that are cold
with nothing but memories
that make us feel old
but you, my love, have given me
more than I could ever ask
life with you is heavenly
no longer a task
for what crosses we may bare
we carry them together
and it doesn't matter
how goes the weather
the joys we discover
are always so new
and I'm so lucky, so blessed
to share them with you
so dry your tears and cry no more
life is waiting for us to live
take my hand and receive God's gift
all of my love to you I give

8:40 PM, Wednesday, October 12, 2011
(for LBL)

Missing You

I'm missing you...

Warm arms that hold me close and tight
Keep me safe all through the night...
Awaken me, your tender kisses delight
With sleepy smiles to greet the sunlight

Gently, my name you caress
In your eyes, no need to guess
Love reigns in our hearts forever
No need to speak or be clever

Just feel, just feel... This is real
Opening my heart, you reveal
Fears I kept so long inside...
Now they are released to die

Rebirthed dreams once forgotten have arrived
Reborn to remind us we are so blissfully alive

Just feel, just feel... Our love is real
In God's presence we shall kneel
Giving thanks to God above
for sending us eternal love

12:01 AM, Tuesday, November 8, 2011
(for LBL)

Feelings

I don't know what to do...
I'm feeling at a loss...
  I'm all mixed up inside
Emotions and words that cross
  Into areas unfamiliar
Unclear and nebular
  I never want to hurt you
Yet somehow I neglect you
  How do I make you understand
I love you more than words
  How do I help you understand
I am freer than all the birds
  I never felt trapped or pigeoned
I give you all I have of me
  You are the best I ever envisioned
Your love came and set me free
  I choose to love you always
And I never want to leave
  Isn't that what I'm meant to do (It's what I want to do)
So why do we grieve?
  Please help me understand
How I can love you best
  Please love me... take my hand
And forget all the rest.

12:12 PM, Wednesday, January 25, 2012

My Wedding Poem to Cynthia

(by Lonnie B. Lamb)

Like the stars in the sky
I am calling to you.

Thru heaven above,
I have looked for you.

In the depths of my soul,
I will live and breathe for you.

You have nothing to fear,
for I am next to you.

Without you
there'd be nothing.
And I could not
seem to see.

Together we are one.
It's no longer
just you or just me.

My heart is love with you.

My soul reaches out to you.

God has sent you to me.

I'll be there if you fall,
to catch you and say I Love You...

And I will love you always.

February 2012

Wedding Vows

What once was friendship has bloomed into love
And I am forever thankful to our Lord God above

For your gentle spirit and loving soul
Has healed my heart and made it whole

I want to pray with you, walk with you, and share
All my love with you, and always show you I care

You honor me with goodness and love that is truly divine
I promise to cherish you and love you until the end of time

What God has shown us is but a taste of His grace
His love is reflected in our joy when we embrace

I love you, Lonnie, always and forever
Te amo, mi amor, por siempre te quiero

February 2012
(for LBL)

Mallard Cove

The ducks have gone
The sun has set
The herons have flown
Now don't you fret

Birds are still singing
The crickets still play
And tomorrow will come
As sure as the dawn becomes day.

The sounds of cars zooming fast
Remind me that sadness
    isn't meant to last.
As airplanes soar to distant lands.
My tears and hurt felt today
    will one day be in the past.

I count my Blessings, I am
    thankful for All
I often lose count and let
    them embrace my fall.

So that when sad thoughts
    beseige me as they
    sometimes will do,

The Blessings God has
    given me will keep
    me from sinking so blue.

cml   5/24/2012

Happy Birthday Mi Amor!
(A poem to you from me)

No fancy graphics, nor e-card here
Just heartfelt wishes that are most sincere
Sending you birthday love and good cheer
For you today and every day of the year

You are more than special, you are truly unique
Your smile brings joy, and the hope that you speak
is reflected in all you do each day of the week
to help and encourage all whom you meet

I am most blessed of all to be your wife
to share with you the rest of our life
God's gift of love manifests through your light
Happy Birthday, my love, my heart's delight!

8:57 AM, Wednesday, June 20, 2012
(for LBL)

Putting the Pieces Together

Digits, bits, pieces...
fragments of feelings memories... Jesus
I love Him for what He did for me,
dying on Calvary to set my soul free

These memories, feelings, fragments...
they sometimes hit me with lament
These pieces, bits, digits...
they nick me, blast me as they hit

And I forget my beauty... I forget I'm free
I'm sometimes then a bit lost in my agony

It's when you smile at me and kiss away my tear
That I can find my way back enough to hear

"I love you."

July 18, 2012
(for LBL)

Love Must Win

Words bristle and emotions flare

Hearts aching to know we care

Fear of rejection, unknown needs

Pain flows in and out despite our deeds

Bruised, bleeding... Past hurts unhealed

Praying, crying, I quietly kneeled

Love must win, love must fight

Love will always conquer the night.

August 28, 2012
(for LBL)

Biographical Notes:

Cynthia M. Lamb has been writing since her maternal grandmother gifted her with her first diary at the age of seven. She began penning poems, cartoons, and short stories in her late teens. A native New Yorker, she has also lived in New Jersey, Pennsylvania, North & South Carolina, Virginia, Louisiana, Puerto Rico, and Florida. Cynthia holds a Bachelor's Degree in Journalism and Spanish from Southern A&M University where she wrote, photographed and edited for the Southern Digest college newspaper. She later wrote for the Daily Advocate newspaper in Baton Rouge, Louisiana, as well as federal newsletters and publications.

Some of her poetry has recently been published in books written by fellow author and friend, Tremayne Moore. Recently retired after a 20-year career in Public Relations and Outreach with the U.S. Department of Agriculture, Cynthia is now pursuing her dream of publishing her own creative works and establishing an editorial business. "Bloom Forever" is a collection of poems written by Cynthia, spanning more than 20 years of her life. It is her first published book. She is an active member of the Tallahassee Authors Network and the Orlando Renaissance Writer's Guild. Cynthia lives in central Florida with her husband, Lonnie, her daughter, Dahlia, and their adopted Jack Russell Terrier- mix, Makayla.

Cynthia is on facebook at: http://www.facebook.com/cmp.lamb

True Love will Bloom Forever... Is nourished with trust, patience, compassion, honesty, loyalty, humor, and faith.

Drawing by CM Lamb

CPSIA information can be obtained at www.ICGtesting.com
Printed in the USA
LVOW071413160213

320398LV00001BA/23/P